BUSH ARTS

MORS KOCHANSKI

LONE
PINE

*For my son Julian and my daughter
Marissa who, more than most
others their age, know
what these crafts
are all about.*

The Publisher:
Lone Pine Publishing
Suite 206
10426-81 Avenue
Edmonton, Alberta
Canada   T6E 1X5

Cover design - Yuet C. Chan
Front cover photos - Bruce Gardave
Back cover photo - Henry Madsen
Illustration - Mors L. Kochanski
Photography - All by Henry Madsen
                 except p. 41 (T. Sittler)
Printing - D. W. Friesen & Sons Ltd.
                 Altona, Manitoba, Canada

Canadian Cataloguing in Publication Data

Kochanski, Mors L.
  Bush arts

  Includes index.
  ISBN 0-919433-49-9

  1. Nature craft. I. Title.
TT157.K62 1988   745.58'4   C88-091600-1

Publisher's Acknowledgement

The publisher gratefully acknowledges the
assistance of the Federal Department of
Communications, Alberta Culture, the Canada
Council, and the Alberta Foundation for the
Literary Arts in the production of this book.

Contents

Preface

The purpose of *Bush Arts* is to provide detailed directions for some of the most popular natural crafts utilizing natural materials commonly found in the world's North Temperate Zone.

These crafts have been chosen because of their appeal and popularity, and because they require only simple tools and use natural materials which are plentiful and readily available. Twenty years of teaching natural crafting assures me that the more than twenty crafts included here will appeal to the young, the old, the novice and the veteran crafter.

No other book that I know of gives the materials of the boreal forest such a universal application. Educator and lay person alike should find much to enjoy and learn in this book.

Mors Kochanski, 1989

Introduction

My first insight into the popularity of natural crafting came early in my career as a survival and wilderness living skills instructor. In the evenings, when the course was over for the day, an individual would begin to carve something and in a short time everyone was doing the same. I instituted carving as an evening pastime mainly to have the students learn how to use a knife more effectively. When students were provided with an appropriate material such as the easily carved black poplar bark, and offered direction — on how to carve a face or "Bannock Gawd", for example — they were ecstatic with the results.

Eventually, I incorporated many other crafts and all elicited a similar response. Once, in gathering sedge for making snare cord and lashing material, as a frivolous aside I demonstrated how quickly a doll could be made with handfuls of grass: something I had read about a few days before. The enthusiasm with which participants immediately made their own dolls led me to teach this craft at every opportunity.

My biggest problem was finding information about local materials which I perceived might have potential crafting applications. Through reading, experimentation and picking the brains of those on my courses who knew more than I did about certain subjects, a file of projects began to form. Eventually, I was able to teach courses devoted to nothing but natural crafting.

This book presents some of the easier, yet very popular, crafts which hold a special place in my heart as they were the earliest ones that I was able to adopt: mainly because of their simplicity and the fact that all can be feasibly made with only a knife.

It is hard to describe adequately the usual reaction of a person making his or her first cattail doll or carving a first face. You can make instant friendships by simply giving people any of the crafts suggested by this book. You will create an even stronger impression by constructing the objects in front of them, and a better one yet if you show them how to make their own.

Early in my career I had the opportunity to teach a class of grade six boys and girls how to make a cattail doll. It soon became apparent that the boys considered doll-making somewhat undignified. First, I sermonized that doll-making would familiarize them with certain properties of the cattail which could have survival applications. The making of the doll, I said, was not the real objective of the exercise, but was rather included to show how a material may be examined and tested for its application in other areas. Then I pointed out that if any of the boys ever wanted to impress a girl who had taken his fancy and cattail was nearby, making a doll and giving it to her would be instantly effective. Many years later one of the boys, as an adult, approached me to explain how he had used this suggestion to his benefit many times over the years.

Painstaking care has been taken to make the directions easy to follow and to understand. The reader is encouraged to read through all steps for a craft before beginning, in order to gain an overall understanding of the project and its variations. Once the idea is mastered, the reader is may add his or her refinements on what has been presented.

Substitution of materials may be carried out to good effect. Cattail leaves can be replaced by yarns, string or strips of cloth, cow parsnip can be replaced by plastic tubing, and so on.

Natural crafting is, above all, meant to be enjoyed.

1 The Tools

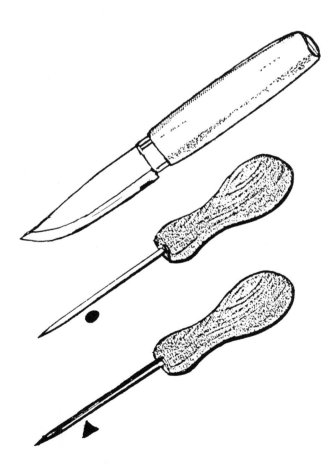

The Knife:
Except for the wreath-maker in Chapter 4, where a saw and a hammer are necessary, the only absolutely essential tool is a sharp knife. A commonly available knife that is highly recommended is the red-handled Mora style that is sold by most hardware and sporting goods stores. The handle should be about as long as your palm and the ideal blade should be shorter than that. A razor-sharp knife is a joy to use, while a dull one makes you work harder and results in cruder work.

Round Awl:
A awl or ice pick (with a round cross section) is an optional tool which is useful in basket weaving and working with the cattail doll. It is helpful in making the moose biscuit (Chapter 6), especially when young people are learning to weave.

Triangular or Square Awl:
These types of awls are used for drilling holes. Where a round awl separates fibers as it penetrates material, the triangular one grinds out a hole. This type of awl is used with wood or bark, particularly for the propeller (Chapter 8) and the Indian head carving (Chapter 10).

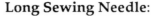

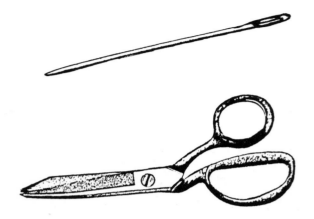

Long Sewing Needle:
A long sewing needle is necessary for the more complex dolls. A needle of seven to ten centimetres will barely be long enough, and one fifteen or more centimetres long would be ideal. The eye should be fairly large to allow for the threading of natural fibers.

Scissors:
For young crafters especially, scissors are safer and more convenient than knives. The paramedic type that will cut tin are recommended.

Safety

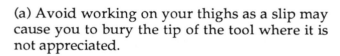

A word on safety is appropriate here. A good rule to follow when first becoming comfortable with the use of any tool is to ask yourself what can happen on the follow-through, when a slip is most likely to occur.

(a) Avoid working on your thighs as a slip may cause you to bury the tip of the tool where it is not appreciated.

(b) Cradling work in the palm of the hand will also result in unsafe follow-through.

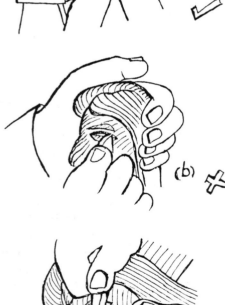

(c) Instead, support your work on a log, bench or table.

Care must be taken while walking with a knife or awl in the hand. If you trip and fall, sharp objects can be driven deep into the body.
When using a knife try to keep the hands clean in case of a cut. Keep an adequate first aid kit at hand.

2 *The Sedge Doll & Whisk*

The Sedge Doll

(a) **The Sedge Doll**:
This doll can be made of any kind of grass and not only of the sedge shown in the picture. This is a crude type of doll which may be made in a few moments. This toy has the advantage in the traditional lifestyle of the Native people that it can be made quickly and as quickly discarded if it is too much trouble to carry to the next camping spot. Those seeing it made for the first time marvel at how a simple material may be configured into a reasonable likeness of a doll in such a short time.

(b)

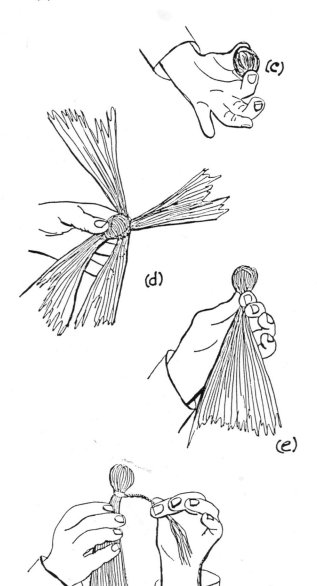

(c)

(d)

(e)

(f)

(b) **The Material:**
The grass shown in the picture is a short-growing sedge commonly found near lake shores. It is tough enough to be twisted into snare cord or strong rope. It can also be used for coiled basketry.

(c) **The Ball or the Brains of the Doll:**
Using pinches of grass, make a ball as if winding up string. Keep winding more grass onto the ball until it is as large as the circle made with the thumb and forefinger (3 or 4 cm). Make the ball more egg-shaped than spherical as the head looks more natural that way.

(d) **The Head Covering:**
The main purpose of the head covering is to produce the neck. Two large pinches of grass are used to cover the ball when the doll is made quickly. Smaller, more numerous pinches may be applied more meticulously for a neater effect.

(e) **The Neck:**
As the covering is applied it is held firmly at the neck at the base of the head, until the covering is complete. The neck may be twisted to tighten the cover even more. Errant strands may be pulled out and discarded.

(f) **The Tie at the Neck:**
The mid-point of a small pinch of grass is wound once or twice around the neck and snugged up by twisting, so that the head-covering is held firmly in place. The twisted ends are tucked into the body to prevent unraveling. If the head is too round, squeeze in the palm of the hand into an oval or egg-shape.

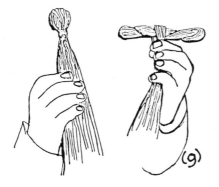

(g) The Arms:
The head and body core are set aside and the arms are made. The arms may be folded or slightly twisted so that the ends meet in the middle. If the arms-component is shaped into a T it will hold its place better in the doll. For a more realistic doll the arms should be as long as the doll is tall. Alternatively, the arms may be seven to eight times the length of the head.

(h) Incorporation of Body and Arms:
Divide the body of the doll into equal parts and insert the arms as far up into the cleft as possible. It is optional at this stage to bind the doll at the waist as was done at the neck.

(i) The Dress or Coat:
Handsful of grass are neatly arranged over the shoulders of the doll until the desirable bulk is achieved. The effect is more pleasing if the doll is made fairly slim. The waistband or belt is made in the initial stage like the tie at the neck. Squeeze the body as the twist is made so that the waist tie is as snug as possible. The twisted end is forced under the belt to complete the tie.

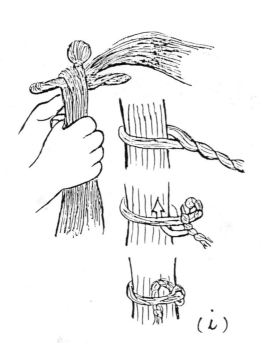

(j) The Completed Doll:
Trim the bottom of the dress. The doll's height should be seven to eight times the length of the head, and the outstretched arms should equal the height of the doll. Trim off any errant blades of grass, and the doll is finished.

The Sedge Whisk

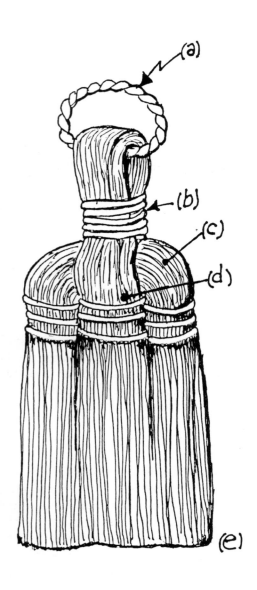

This is a simple, neat project that displays nicely when hung on a wall. The sedge pictured near the beginning of this chapter is a good material for the construction of this broom. Soften the grass by dampening it and letting it sit overnight in a plastic bag.

(a) **The Ring**:
This is made with a spruce root (see Chapter 9) wound around itself into a ring, with the ends hidden in the fold of the handle.

(b) **The Handle Whipping**:
Whipping is described in the construction of the simple cattail doll (Chapter 3).

(c) **The Outer Bristles**:
The bulk of the outside bristles equals the bulk of the central portion of the broom.

(d) **The Frapping**:
This is made with fresh or well-soaked spruce roots. First make the turns loosely and then pull them tight. Let the broom dry thoroughly before use to set the spruce root.

(e) **Trimming**:
The bristles are trimmed off and the project is complete.

3 *The Cattail Doll*

The cattail doll in its many forms is one of the most universally popular natural crafts. This type differs from the corn husk doll in that cattail leaves are longer and coarser and wire is not usually used in shaping the body.

Cattail Leaves

There are two types of cattail plant, the seed-bearing and the vegetative. The seed-bearing plant sports the familiar mace or head and the vegetative one consists entirely of leaves. The shaft (**S**) of the seed-bearing plant has many applications. In this book it is used for a broom handle, as a slide handle in the trombone whistle, and as sticks of firewood carried by a doll.

The leaves from the seed-bearing stalk are seldom used as they are inferior in shape or length compared to those of the vegetative stalk. The leaves in the vegetative stalk can be classified as follows:

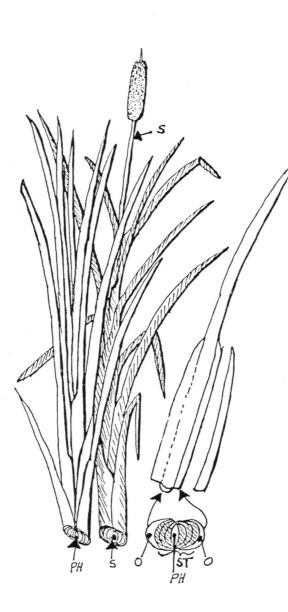

Outside leaves (O):

These are the shortest, broadest and generally the thinnest on any given stalk. Because of their rarity, the finest quality broad leaves should be saved for special applications such as head coverings, dresses, aprons and angel wings. To better flatten a leaf, cut the skin on its concave side by scratching its surface with the tip of a knife or awl. The edges of these broad leaves which are thin and tough are especially useful as a stitching material, for use with a needle.

Standard leaves (ST):

These leaves comprise the greatest number (about six) in any given stalk. They are concave on one side and convex on the other.

Prime heart leaf (PH):

There is only one leaf in the heart of the vegetative stalk that is convex on both sides of the blade. This leaf can be split in half on the long axis for applications where thinness is required, such as in the bindings used to make feet or boots in some dolls. This is the strongest and most supple leaf in the stalk. The heart leaf also makes the finest braids.

Leaf variations:

It is suggested that you become familiar with the cattails growing over a wide range. In certain areas you may find plants that have particularly broad leaves at their bases. In other areas the plants may have a leaf which is narrower than usual, or more delicate or silkily textured than normal. Cattails growing in sheltered locations are more workable than those found in the open. About an eighth of the plants gathered should be as small as possible and an equal amount should be as large as possible. With time, you will find that a wide selection of leaf sizes and types will allow you to create a better looking product.

Harvesting Cattail:

For the applications described in this book, a good time to gather cattail is in the fall as soon as the plant has turned brown. By mid-winter the leaves may be so deteriorated from weathering by wind and sun that they become sodden rather than soft when soaked. They also become more fragile. Gather the leaves when they can be folded into bundles of a size that can be easily stuffed into large a plastic bag. Ideally, this should be done after a rain when the leaves are supple enough to fold without cracking. The leaves should be dried for storage or they will mould. Properly stored, they will remain suitable for crafting for years. They should be well soaked and perhaps wrapped with an old towel or cotton shirt and kept in a plastic bag for a day or two before use, for maximum pliability.

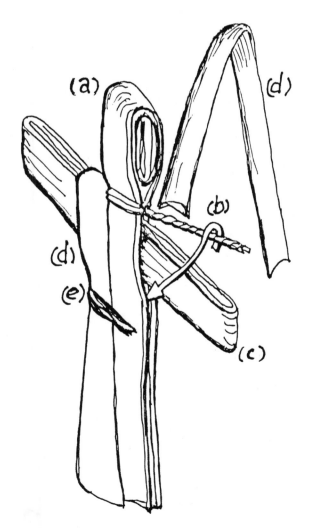

The Simple Doll

The simple doll is one that a pre-schooler can make. It is made in much the same way as the sedge doll described earlier.

(a) To make the head, neck and body core, a leaf is rolled into an oval form and covered with another leaf or two.

(b) For the tie at the neck split a small leaf down the middle, wrap its middle portion once or twice around the neck and twist the ends together until the tie is snug. Tuck the twisted end into the body core to prevent its unravelling.

(c) For the arms, a leaf is folded as shown so that it equals the height of the doll, and its ends are hidden in the body core.

(d) For a coat, a few leaves are placed over each shoulder.

(e) The waist is bound like the neck but the twisted end is tucked under the waist binding. Trim the doll to complete it.

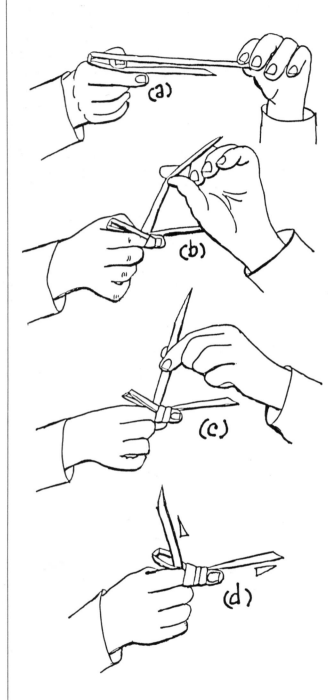

Whipping

A more sophisticated method of binding at the neck and waist is by whipping. Tying knots in a cattail leaf usually breaks it whereas whipping allows the use of the full strength of the leaf. Tight whipping at the neck and waist are necessary for a good looking doll.

Practice whipping on your forefinger or a bundle of leaves until you become proficient at it.

(a) Make a fold as shown, leaving enough of the short end to be able to pull on it later.

(b) Begin wrapping, making the first wrap quite snug.

(c) Wrap as many turns as required.

(d) Lock the whip by passing the winding end through the loop without allowing the wrappings to loosen, and pull on the short end to close the loop completely.

(e) The ends may be trimmed off. For the tie at the neck these ends are simply incorporated into the body core. For the waist tie, the ends may be twisted into a waist cord or a third equal-sized strand taken from the doll's dress and the three elements braided together.

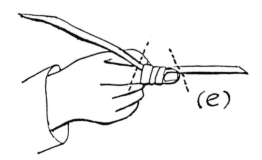

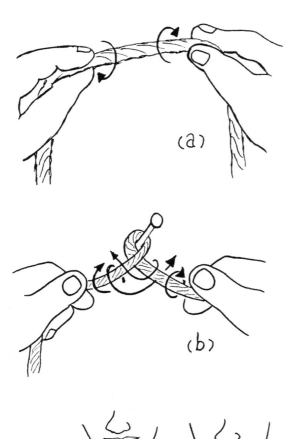

Twisting

It may also be useful to practice twisting rope beforehand. This technique is used to make doll's arms, octopus tentacles and waist sashes.

(a) Twist a leaf at its midpoint (clockwise) until a kink appears. This is the beginning of the "rope."

(b) Put this kink over a nail, or grasp it with your teeth and without letting the twists unwind make them go around each other in a counter-clockwise direction. After repeating this step a number of times you should have a distinct piece of rope that does not unwind.

(c) If you have done your twisting incorrectly, your cord will not look like a rope and it will not hold together. Both strands must be twisted in the same direction and then around each other in the opposite direction.

(d) To prevent unravelling after you have finished, make a half hitch as if to tie a knot.

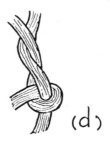

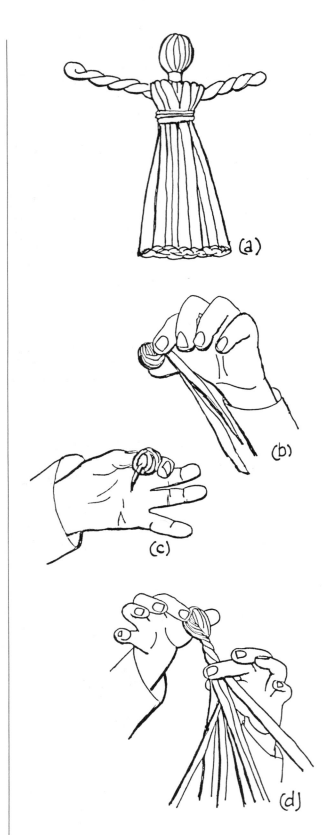

The Standard Doll

The standard doll is the simple unembellished form that is the starting point for all the more complex ones that follow.

(a) This is what this doll looks like. It requires about six vegetative cattail stalks, of which one is smaller and one is larger than the average.

(b) The brains of the doll are two standard size leaves that are wound into a ball, as if winding string. As the head should be more an egg shape than spherical, squeeze the ball now and again to make it more oval. To produce the most pleasing effect it is necessary to match the size of the leaf to the size of doll: making a big doll out of leaves that are too small or making a small doll out of leaves that are too big tends to create an awkward effect. Trial and error has determined that the size of head that results from using two standard size leaves is a good rule of thumb for matching the size of doll to the size of leaf.

(c) The completed ball is one-seventh to one-eighth the height of the doll.

(d) The ball is now covered with about six smaller or narrower-than-average leaves as these tend to produce a better effect.

All are made to cross at the very top of the head and are overlapped so that the ball is covered neatly and completely. Once this is done the neck is twisted slightly to tighten the covering leaves a little more. The neck is then whipped with a prime heart leaf. If the head is too round, squeeze it into a more oval shape.

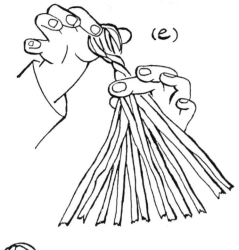

(e) **Octopus**: At this stage an octopus may be made. Use ten more leaves in covering the head and whip as before. This will provide four leaves for each tentacle.

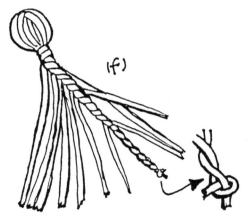

(f) With two leaves to a strand, twist two strands together to make a rope one third the desired length of a tentacle. Then exclude about a third of the bulk of each strand and twist the remaining material for another third of the length. Finally, remove half the bulk of each strand and twist together what remains, finishing with a half hitch to prevent unravelling. This gradual thinning is called rat-tailing. Do the remaining tentacles in the same way.

(g) To continue with the doll proper omit steps "e" and "f". Using the finger widths, roughly measure out seven head lengths and trim off the excess.

(h) Gather six to eight of the longest standard leaves, with half of the leaves lying in an opposite direction to the other half so that the bundle of leaves will tend to be of a consistent thickness throughout. This bundle should be about four times as long as the doll is tall. At a point one third from an end begin twisting the first arm.

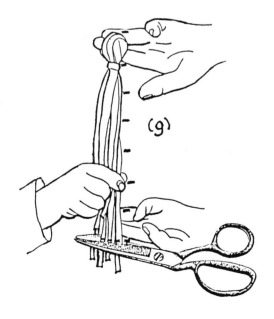

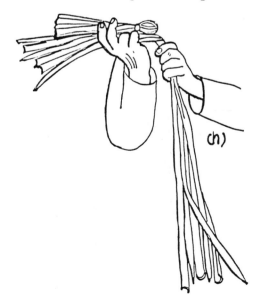

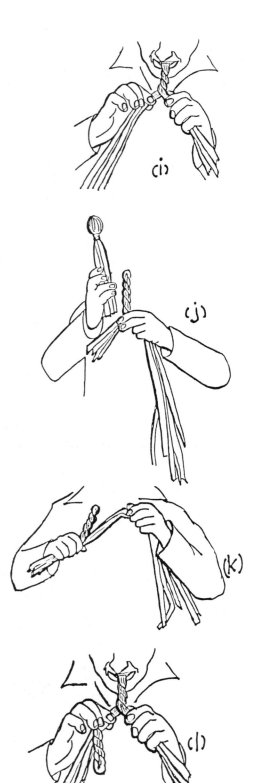

(i) About seven twists will produce a length of arm that is half the height of the doll. One of the leaves in the short end of the bundle may be used to make a tie that will keep the rope from unravelling while the second arm is made.

(j) The length of the arm should be about half the height of the doll.

(k) Taking the long end of the bundle and folding it alongside the completed arm, locate the point one quarter longer than the completed arm from which to start twisting the second arm.

(l) Twist until the base of the first arm is reached.

(m) The completed arms should form a T.

(n) Part the body core in the middle and insert the arms. Fold leaves over each shoulder until a desired bulk is achieved. Whip at the waist. Trim the bottom of the dress. The standard doll shown at (a) is now complete.

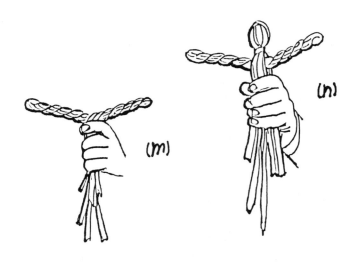

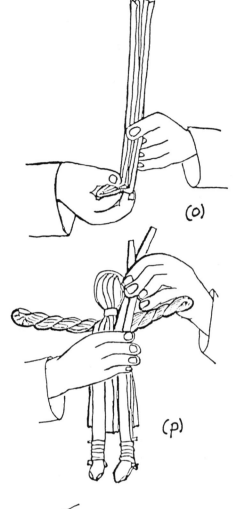

Variations

(o) **Adding feet:** Trial and error will determine how many leaves are necessary for making the leg and foot. The central portion of the leaf bundle is folded into an outline of a foot. The length of the foot is about the length of the head. A split heart leaf is used to bind the foot so that it retains its configuration. An end of the binding leaf is inserted between the leaves at the start and at the finish.

(p) The legs are anchored to the body with the far ends being folded over the shoulders.

(q) The dress or outer coat is put on.

(r) The doll is whipped firmly at the waist.

(s) Braids may be added by folding one continuous braid over the top of the head. For an added refinement, make the part of the braid over the top of the head loose enough to insert a fold of leaf to form the bangs.

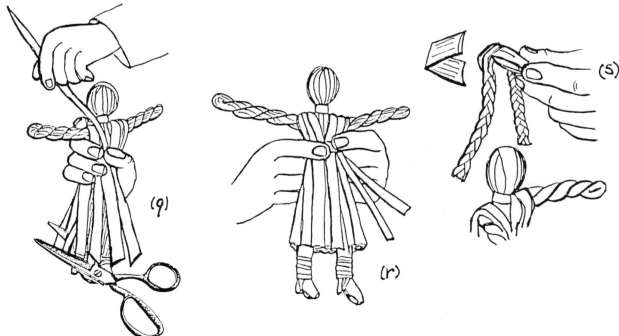

(t)

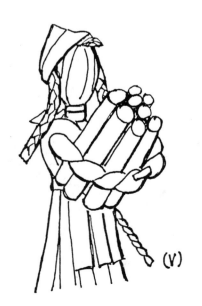

(u)

(t) The head is covered with a head shawl which is tied on at the neck with leaf edging. The completed doll is shown.

(u) To make the broom, fold a large, long leaf into a flat roll and cut one end of the roll off. Poke a hole in the other end with a knife tip and insert the handle. The broom head is then whipped to hold it on to the handle and the bristles are made with a knife tip. The handle may be made from the seed-bearing stalk or a willow wand. Leave the handle extra long until it has been fitted in the doll's hands and then trim it to size. The twisted arms with their 'fists' have an excellent gripping action.

(v) This doll is made to carry an armful of wood. The hands are stitched together and the space formed by the circle of the arms is stuffed with pieces of cattail stem.

(w) To make it appear as though a doll is cradling a baby in its arms, one arm is made about a quarter-arm-length longer than the other and a ball representing the baby's face is incorporated at its tip. This arm is then wrapped around the other one, as shown, to complete the effect.

(v)

(w)

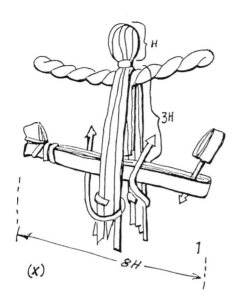

(x)

(a)

(x) The Sitting Doll: The legs are a few folds of a long leaf or two, made as long as the outstretched arms. The legs join the body at the halfway point of the height of the doll. When the legs are inserted, the front part of the body core is folded back and the back is folded forward. The waist is whipped to hold everything in place. A coat may now be added in the usual way.

The Kitchen or Hallowe'en Witch

The kitchen witch is the most popular of the cattail dolls. The hair is old man's beard (*Alectoria*) and the hat is made of birch bark. The thread used to sew the hat together is made of stinging nettle fiber.

(a) The doll in this figure was well soaked and then trussed up in a tight sitting position. After the doll is dry, the binding is removed and the doll should maintain a sitting posture while riding her broom. The components of her hat are shown. The hole in the brim part fits snugly on the head.

(b) The conical part of the hat is stitched so that it holds its form.

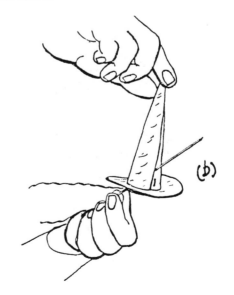

(b)

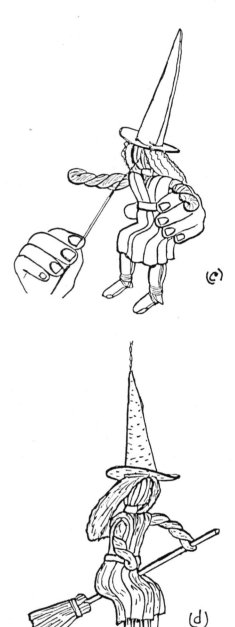

(c)

(d)

(c) The hair is put on the head and the hat is firmly stitched on to the head. The thread for hanging the doll is strung through the tip of the cone.

(d) A hole is made through the dress for inserting the broom to achieve the impression that the doll is sitting on it or straddling it.

The Cattail Angel

(e) The cattail angel is a standard doll having wings and a halo. Some broad leaves are folded and trimmed as shown in the diagram to form the wings. The halo is a long braid formed in a loop behind the head. The wings and the halo are both stitched on at the same time with leaf edging. Small angels are used as Christmas tree ornaments and large ones may be incorporated into wreaths (see Chapter 4).

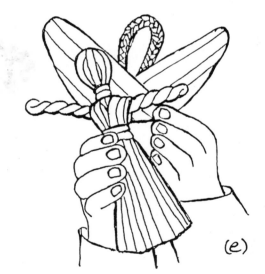

(e)

4 *The Christmas Wreath*

The Christmas wreath made of local natural materials has a special appeal. The northern forests provide many materials attractive enough to be used in wreaths, but only a few of these are long and supple enough to be used directly, without a wreath-maker. A wreath-maker will allow you put together these shorter materials and hold them in place until they are bound together.

(a)

(a) The completed wreath.
The picture shows a wreath constructed with the use of the wreath-maker described in this chapter. The wreath is made of the same sedge used in making the doll in Chapter 1. The fringe is made of sprigs of green labrador tea and red rose hips that add color to the wreath.

(b) Constructing the Wreath-maker
Whatever materials you choose may be packed into a wreath-maker. To keep the materials in place, nails are inserted into the appropriate holes. When a fringe is being incorporated, courser, more available or less valuable materials may be used to build up the back of the wreath. The fringe elements are kept in place under the nails in the lower holes. Where a simple unadorned

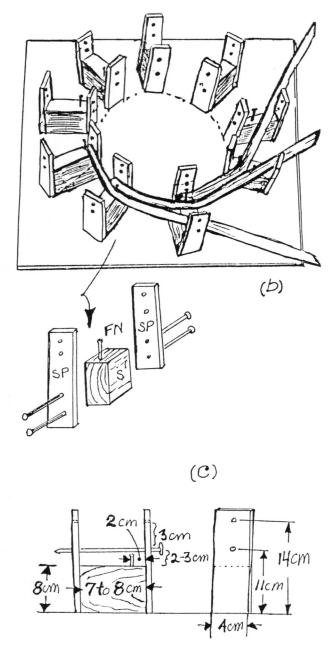

(b)

(c)

ring is wanted the lower portion is all that is used. The second hole is used when you want to make a more complex or fancy facing, particularly if you are working with cattail.

The inside diameter of the wreath-maker is 25 cm. The width of the ring is about 7 to 8 cm. Nine retaining units are shown in the diagram. The number used is determined by the space that must be made between them to allow the spool of string, used to bind the wreath, to pass freely between them. A space of about 4 cm is about right.

(c) The retaining unit

The spacer block **(S)** is a piece of two-by-four that is as long as the desired width of ring. A nail is driven into the block about 2 cm from the inside edge of the circle just short enough to allow the lower retaining nail to clear it. The side pieces of the retaining unit are nailed or screwed on to the spacer block. This may be molding or pieces of plywood of about the same width as the spacer block is thick. The lower hole is 3 cm and the upper is 6 cm from the top surface of the spacer block. The holes for the retaining nails are made big enough for the nails you have available. Assemble about a dozen retaining units.

The base of the wreath-maker may be a piece of plywood or may be made out of boards. As a guide draw an inside circle with a diameter of about 25 cm, or whatever you desire, and install the retaining units with a space of not less than 4 cm between them.

Set up the wreath-maker at about chair-seat height, so that you can work at it while seated, and you are ready for production.

Wreath Materials:

The most versatile and pliable material to use is cattail, but anything that is not too stiff may prove suitable. Try whatever is found in abundance in your vicinity. Other wilderness materials that have been used to good effect are twining honeysuckle, bracted honeysuckle, red osier dogwood, buffalo berry, tamarack twigs, dwarf birch, shrubby cinquefoil, canary grass, various sedges or slough grasses, bullrush and balsam

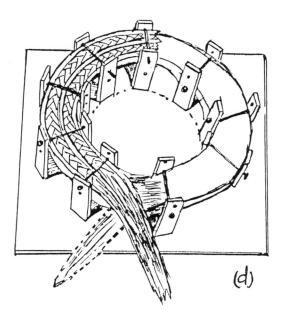

(d)

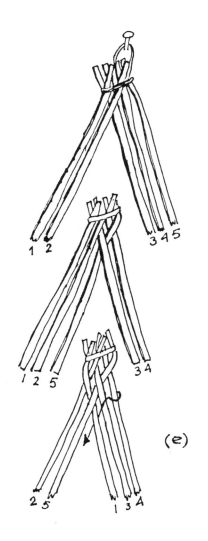

(e)

fir boughs. Domestic materials such as straw, the various grains with the heads still on, hop vines, pea vines and garden flowers that have to be uprooted in the fall, such as bachelor's buttons, all make good wreaths.

The two basic considerations in wreath making are texture and color. Bright, eye-catching colors are not common in nature. Two exceptions are the red of rose hips and the green of labrador tea, two appropriate Christmas colors.

Many wreaths found on the commercial market derive their texture from vine-like materials. The one natural material that resembles grape vines is twining honeysuckle. Although it is not a rare plant, wreath-making could make it so. Make the core of the wreath from something more common such as cattail, and use honeysuckle only for the surface. The same applies to tamarack, which provides a special knobby texture.

Cattail in itself provides a pleasing texture but it may also be given different textures by braiding and twining. A rope can be made out of cattail and coiled to cover the front surface of the wreath. Wide and narrow braids can also be used. The size of wreath presented in this book will be accommodated nicely by two average-length vegetative cattail stalks, each of which will go around half the wreath's circumference. Diagram (d) clarifies this point. Braids should be long enough to reach half way around the wreath. The thick ends of both braids are wedged under the top retaining nail at the top of the wreath. For braids that do not cover the full width of the wreath, linings or edgings of cattail stalk may be used. What is left over at the bottom of the wreath may be trimmed off or left to hang down.

(e) **Braiding**

Most people can braid with three elements. Where wider braids are required one may easily use seven elements. Using odd numbers of elements makes it easier to keep track of where you are, which will keep your braiding straight.

To make a five-element braid take five vegetative cattail stalks and remove the outer leaves until something of thumb-thickness remains. Tie the thick ends together with cord so that you can

(f)

anchor the beginning of the braid to some object. Hold two elements in one hand and three in the other. Take the topmost element of the greatest number (3 as opposed to 2) and go over, then under, so that this element is now parallel to the two in the opposite hand. Now the topmost of the greatest number is on the opposite side and this element is made to go over, then under. The braid is continued in this way, always working with the highest element of the greatest number. A seven-element braid would have three elements in one hand and four in the other and the weaving would go over, under, over.

(f) This picture shows the beginning of the wreath shown at the head of the chapter. Small handfuls of sedge of a consistent size are systematically wedged in the narrow space behind the nail in each retaining unit. This will produce a ring of a consistent thickness.

(g)

(g) Sprigs of labrador tea, rose hips, alder branches with cones and tamarack twigs are wedged under the lower nail at each retaining unit. More sedge will now be incorporated , which will be held in place by the higher nails. A fine, strong string is then used to tie the wreath together. A loop is tied in the end of the string and hooked over one of the nails. The string is wrapped as tightly as possible short of breaking it, taking a turn in the gap between the retaining units and then passing over the top of the retaining unit on the next turn. Pull out the retaining nails in turn as you cross each retaining unit. When the nail holding the looped end of the string is reached, it is removed and the ends of the string tied together. The wreath can now be extracted from the wreath-maker.

The most suitable string is either brown or black in color. This can be kite string, sail-making thread or heavy nylon sewing thread. Some synthetic yarns are very strong and are suitable for this purpose. A combination of a red, white and green yarn may produce a nice effect.

Once you gain the basics behind the use of the wreath-maker you may find the possibilities limitless.

5 The Tamarack Twig Bird or Decoy

Tamarack branch tips are readily formed into the shapes of birds. The Canada goose decoy made by the Native people of some parts of Northern Canada is familiar to many. The bird described in this article, a simplified version of the real thing, is not meant to be a decoy, but an ornament. The large decoy takes hours to make as its binding is stitched with a sail needle. This version is made with one continuous winding of string, without the use of a needle, in a matter of minutes.

These birds can be made with fine twigs other than tamarack, such as dwarf birch and willow. The advantage of tamarack over other materials is that the knobby nature of the twigs helps to hold windings in place, and their extraordinary suppleness allows the branches to be more easily molded into desired shapes. Tamarack also emits a pleasant fragrance while it dries that can be freshened a little by sprinkling with water. Other twigs may be used, depending on the ease with which the string may be embedded in their bark to hold it in place. The main problem area is the transition from body to neck, where the binding string tends to 'fall off' and loosen.

(a)

(b)

(a) Examples of birds made of tamarack:
These birds are displayed on a patch of snow. Note how the snow showing through the 'eye' could represent the white cheek-patch of the Canada goose. A standing bird can have one leg if the ground or snow will allow poking a stick into it; otherwise, three legs are used. Native people maintain that Canada geese do not know how to count legs.

(b) Arrangement of materials to make the bird:
The body core of the bird is an oblong ball that may be made of tamarack twigs, grass or cattail. The outer covering of the bird is a bundle of twigs with all the thick ends at one end. This is firmly bound to form the tail end. The quantity of twigs should be such that there are enough to cover the ball completely. Long unbranched twigs produce the finest results, but this type of twig is not found everywhere.

(c) The core is forced into the bundle:
Determine the center of the bundle and force the core well against the tail binding for short-tailed birds, less so for long-tailed ones.

(c)

(d)

(d) Binding the tail and body:
Shape the body and begin wrapping with the string starting at the tail. Squeeze tightly at the neck to give it a graceful shape.

(e) The first step in shaping the head:
The head is made by dividing the twigs into two parts; the lower jaw and the upper part of the head. The lower jaw may be wound first and backtracked to wind the upper part.

(e)

(f) The beak:
The upper and lower parts are brought together and the binding of the beak completed and tied off to finish the head.

(g) The completed bird:
If the tail were trimmed off much shorter, this would look more like a water fowl. Sometimes it may be necessary to unwind the tail and do it over again in reverse. To help the bird stand on a flat surface, two short pegs are forced into its breast. Trim off any twigs that are out of place.

Fine twigs may be used to make birds with bodies that are about the size of hens' eggs. These may be used in making attractive mobiles that simulate a swimming action on the part of the birds.

(f)

(g)

Mobiles

Mobiles are animated works of art that have a definite application in natural crafting. Anything involved with motion immediately lends itself to mobile application. Miniature decoys, flying birds, coasters, and cattail dolls are readily incorporated into mobiles as a special effect. The eye-catching movement of a well-made mobile will add life to a dull corner of a room. Hung over a child's bed, it can provide a great stimulus to the sight and the imagination.

Mobiles can be the subject of a book in themselves. They can be as simple or as complex as desire dictates. Creating mobiles suitable to natural crafting applications depends heavily on trial and error.

The basic principles of mobile design are quite simple, and are an alternative application for some of the projects covered in the book. They tend to fill either horizontal or vertical space. A mother goose swimming with her goslings, for example, would appropriately fill a horizontal space. Fish swimming around each other might better fill a vertical space. Mobiles are constructed from the bottom up, starting with the smallest elements.

6 *The Moose Biscuit or Hot Pot Mat*

There are at least eight basket weaving materials that can be found in the northern forests. Red osier dogwood ranks high because of its availability, ease of use and its colorful and pleasing appearance.

(a) **Red osier dogwood in blossom:**
The best time to weave with red osier dogwood is when the plant has dropped its leaves. When the leaves are on it, the weavers tend to be very weak at the leaf joints. The weavers become more supple through wilting if stored in a warm place for a day or two before use. If the weavers dry out they are ruined as they cannot be softened again by soaking.

The shoots that are so highly esteemed for weaving are equally esteemed by moose as forage. A moose may consume over 25 kg of red osier dogwood daily. This is why this sometimes slender and densely growing plant is called 'moose spaghetti'. Since this project is a round hot-pot mat, it seems appropriate to call it a moose biscuit.

The moose biscuit is a good introduction to basket weaving with wands as it is in essence the bottom and the rim of a basket. Spruce roots or willow wands can be substituted for red osier dogwood.

(b) Sorting the weavers:
Gather about 200 wands which are free of any branches, ranging in length from about half a metre to a metre. Sort into six or seven sizes by grasping the longer wands each in turn and shaking them out of the bundle.

(c) The weavers laid out:
To create a neater effect and a firmer weave, start with a fine, more flexible weaver followed by progressively larger ones. Laid out in front of the weavers are the thicker wands that will be used for spokes. These wands are about as thick as a pencil and may have to be taken from branched wands. If the spokes are so thin that they bend during weaving or if the spokes are too thick, the work will look ugly.

(d) Preparing the spokes:
Of the spoke material cut out six closely matched sticks that are about a hand-span or more long, and one stick half the length. Pierce three of the thicker sticks with a knife or awl as shown.

(e) Assembling the spokes:
Force the three remaining spokes into the slot made in (d) and insert the half spoke as shown. Without the half spoke introducing a odd number of spokes, the weaving would not alternate sides with each circuit around in weaving (termed a stroke).

(f) Introducing the first weaver:
Start with the thin end of a thin weaver which will better stand the severe bending required at this stage. This is the only instance where a weaver is started with the thin end. Starting with a thick end and finishing with a thin end produces a neater result. A new weaver is started by jamming in its thick end beside the spoke that is three spokes ahead of the point where the previous weaver has ended. Decide which side of the mat is to be the off side and have all weaving end on this side. The finger pressure technique shown in the picture helps to keep the weavers from cracking.

(g) Weaving continued:
Each following weaver should be slightly larger than the previous one. Here the point has been reached where a spoke should be separated away from each group of three. This is done when the weavers do not want to lie firmly against the spokes and there is some room next to the spoke for it to bend. Alternatively, you can separate spokes when the weaving reaches the point where there is a two-finger space between spokes. When a separation is made, revert back to a thinner weaver again. Continue weaving until the paired spokes are separated and the weaving progresses to the point where there is about a two-finger space between all the single spokes.

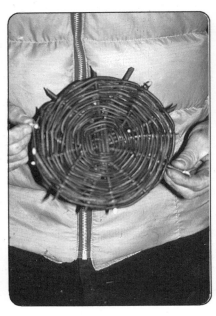

(h) **Consolidation weave**:
Two of the longest weavers are inserted next to adjacent spokes and are woven simultaneously around each other and the spokes, until the weavers are used up. This is a solid type of weave that will hold the rim in place better for the following steps.

(i) **Body of mat completed**:
The consolidation weave is completed. Using a knife, the protruding ends should be trimmed off flush with the weaving.

(j) **Sorting the weavers for the rim**:
There will be three weavers required for each spoke. As there are thirteen spokes, 39 weavers are required. The more uniform the weavers are in thickness, the neater the effect. By gathering the weavers even with their thin ends, a close match may be made.

(k) **Trimming the rim weavers**:
Trim all the thick ends off at the shortest end in the bundle. Trim off some of the soft ends.

(l) Inserting the spokes:
Insert three weavers at each spoke. If the spaces between the spokes are not equal, insert the weavers on the side of the spoke that will tend to correct the problem. Insert the single weaver on the side of the narrower gap and the pair on the side of the wider gap.

(m) Weaving the rim:
Without kinking any of the weavers start weaving the rim by taking the three weavers at one of the spokes and passing them behind the adjacent three, in front of the next and behind the third set, ending on the off side. Note that this first weave is not made tightly against the rim, leaving room for weaving when the circuit is nearly completed.

(n) Weaving continued:
Continue to weave in the same manner as in (m). Keep the groups of three as flat as possible.

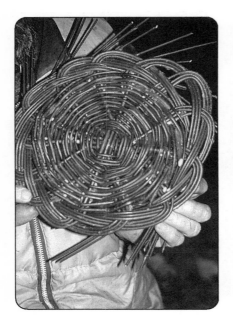

(o) **Rim completed**:
When the last two spokes are reached, continue the same weaving pattern of behind, in front, behind as usual even though the weavers are already incorporated in the rim. Close any holes or gaps by pulling on the appropriate weavers.

(p) **Trimming**:
Let the moose biscuit dry for a few days or some of the weavers may pop out of place when they are trimmed close to the weaving.

(q) The completed moose biscuit.

7 Cow Parsnip & Willow Whistles

Cow parsnip is one of the few hollow-stemmed plants to be found in the northern forests. The plant is usable only when it is dead and dry, as the smell of the freshly cut plant is unpleasant and overpowering.

(a) **The mature plant:**
Cow parsnip prefers rich, disturbed soil which accounts for the plant's being commonly found along roadsides. This plant should not be confused with water hemlock which has narrow leaves and a spherical configuration of the seed head: cow parsnip has huge rhubarb-like leaves and a flat-topped seed head.

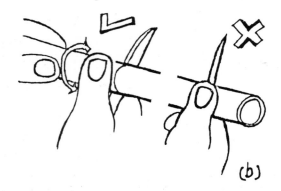

(b)

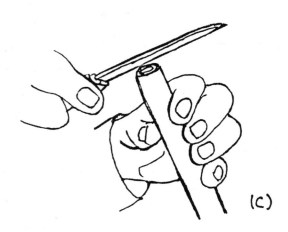

(c)

(d)

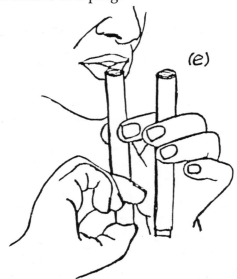

(e)

(b) Sectioning cow parsnip:
For a clean break, cow parsnip must be scored with a knife and then snapped. Hold the thumb to the side as you roll the stem between thumb and knife-edge to prevent a cut.

(c) Flattening sharpies:
The end of the tube usually has sharp projections that can be flattened with the side of the knife blade. Swelling may result if these projections are not removed and later penetrate the skin of the lips.

(d) Testing for air leakage:
A tube with holes or cracks in it is useless for whistle-making. The easiest method to test for this is to subject the tube to air pressure with the mouth. Wherever there is a leaf coming off the stem there is a blockage of the tube, called a node. The crude forms of whistle require a closed tube to make them work. An open-end whistle has to be twice as long as a closed-end whistle for the same note.

(e) Simplest whistle:
The simplest whistle is a closed tube that is made to work by blowing across the top of the opening. For a straight tube, the far end may be closed off with the thumb or a plug.

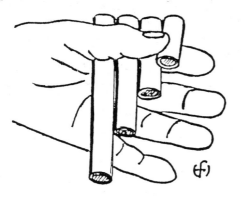

(f) Pan pipe:
Tubes of various lengths can be simply held or lashed together for the more conventional pan pipe. The ends of the tubes have been closed with willow plugs.

(g) A two tone whistle:
Using a section with a node in it, make the short end quite shrill and the other end of a more pleasant tone. Poke a tiny hole through the node as shown in the cross-section. Too big a hole will spoil the whistle. Blow over the long end as you open and close the other end with your thumb.

(h) Japanese whistle:
An oblique cut on the end of the tube allows you to blow in line with it, which is easier to blow than over the flat end.

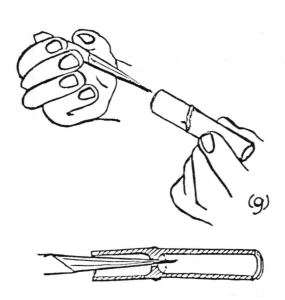

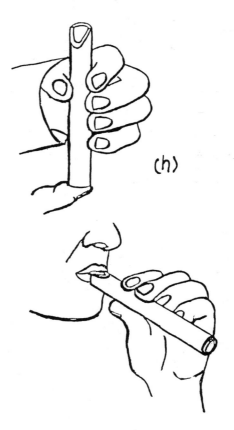

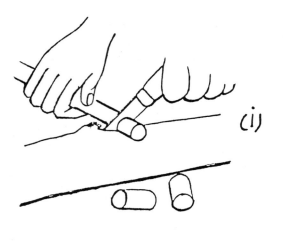

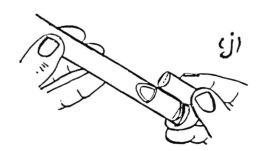

(i) **Cutting plugs for the common whistle:**
Peel willow sticks of a wide range of diameters and use this shear arrangement with a knife to cut large numbers of plugs. The plugs should be at least two centimetres long to stay wedged in the tube end of the whistle.

(j) **Matching the plug to a given bore:**
If the plug is too loose it will fall out. If it is too tight it may split the whistle. Binding the end with thread helps prevent splitting. This system is recommended when children are learning to make this whistle.

(k) **Splitting the plug:**
Splitting off a piece of the plug to make the wind channel may result in a cut to the hand. A safe method is to lightly set the knife blade where the split is desired and complete the cut by tapping on a solid object.

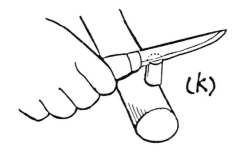

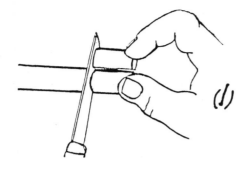
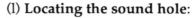

(l) Locating the sound hole:
If the plug is not to protrude take a measure where the back edge of the hole is to be.

(m) Cutting the lip:
The knife must be sharp to cut a proper lip. If the hole is too small the whistle must be blown very gently to produce a sound. If the hole is too big it will need to be blown hard to get a sound.

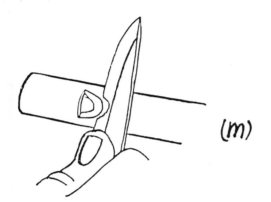

(n) The wind channel:
The wind channel must be even with the bottom of the hole. The end of the plug is usually even with the vertical cut of the whistle hole.

(o) Tuning:
Start with the end of the plug flush with the vertical cut of the hole. Push the plug toward the lip until the best sound is produced. This is a loud, crude whistle which only works if the far end is closed.

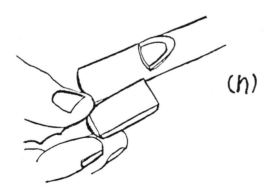
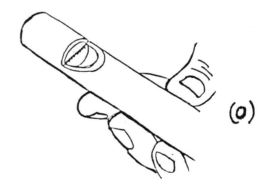

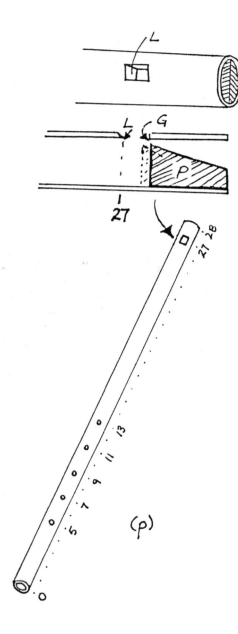

(p)

(p) The finger flute:

It is relatively easy to make a flute if the whistle part is made correctly. This requires a very sharp knife and some attention to detail. The whistle hole must be cut as shown in the diagram. The lip (**L**) must be as sharp as possible. The wind channel must be very narrow at the gap (**G**). The plug should be cut with a slope to achieve adequate blast, and its best position is determined by sliding it back and forth. By trial and error you may locate a few finger holes that will produce distinct notes.

For a long flute find a tube that has a bore that can accommodate the middle finger in the small end and is at least thirty diameters long. Make a whistle in the big end in the manner that has just been described. From the lip measure 27 diameters and cut the tube to length. Drill or carve holes (square or round) at 5, 7, 9, 11, and 13 diameter distances from the open end.

(q) Slides for a trombone whistle:

The trombone whistle never fails to delight those that see it for the first time. The slides may be made in different ways. (1) the simplest and most effective is to use a small seed- bearing cattail stalk. (2) A section from a vegetative cattail stalk can be impaled on a sharpened willow rod and tightly whipped at the base. (3) Old man's beard may be wrapped on a split end of a willow rod (see detail). (4) When nothing else is available a wad of kleenex covered with polyethylene and whipped onto the end of a willow rod will do.

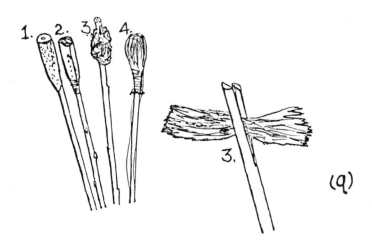

(q)

(r) Trombone whistle in use:
All the whistle ends described in this chapter can be used with the trombone or slide whistle. To make the whistle work properly, the piston of the slide must fit closely and be sealed with water or cooking oil while in use.

(s) Other artifacts made from cow parsnip:
The stalk makes an excellent blowgun pipe. The projectiles (for play) may be (1) berries of various sorts, (2) willow plugs, (3) sections of cattail head, (4) a dart with carved fletching and (5) a dart with thistle-down fletching bound on with thread.

Klondikers made gold dust containers out of cow parsnip stalks. The plug end is bound with thread to prevent it from cracking. In survival fishing the stalk can be used as a bait container for grasshoppers and bees. These are pushed down into the container with a thin rod. The sides are broken away until the bait is reached. The bait is then hooked and the plug is replaced.

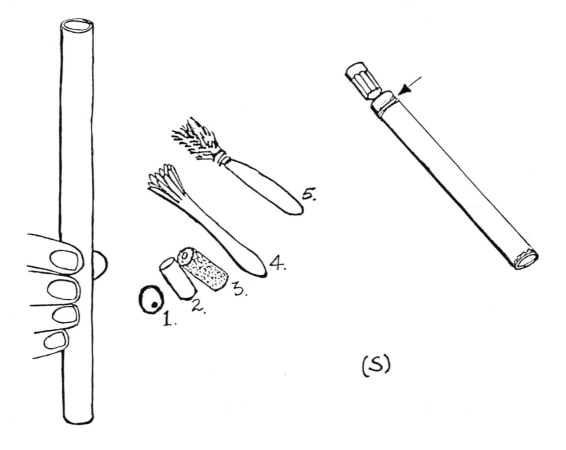

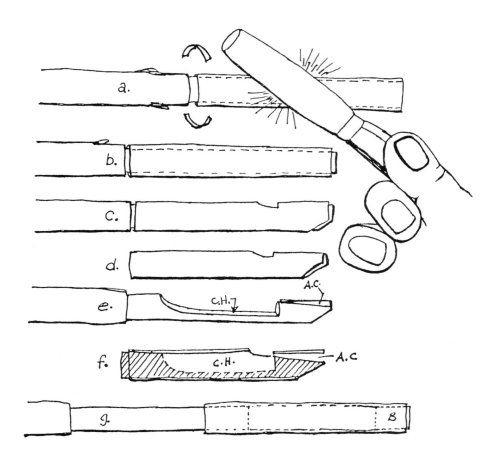

The Willow Whistle

When the sap rises in the willow from about mid-May to early July, the bark can be loosened from the wood. Locate a straight knot-free section no longer than your palm, and thicker than the little finger. Adjacent to this in the direction of the thicker part of the willow leave enough length to act as a handle when twisting off the bark.

(a) Remove about a half centimetre of bark. If this does not come off easily, it will be impossible to remove the bark. Gently tap the bark from end to end and all the way around. Try to twist the bark loose. You may have to repeat the tapping, but just a little harder each time. Tapping too hard may crack the bark and ruin the whistle.

(b) Remove the bark to see if it is undamaged. Replace the bark and close the testing gap slightly.

(c) Cut the lip of the whistle by cutting away the bark and a little of the wood.

(d) Remove the bark.

(e) Cut the air channel (AC) and the chamber (CH).

(f) Cut off the handle and replace the bark. Tune, and the whistle is ready for use.

(g) The pop gun. The pop gun never fails to make a big hit. Cut a section off the end of the plunger to make the bullet. Withdraw the plunger and moisten it slightly in your mouth. Moisten the bullet as well before use. This gun should produce a very audible

8 *The Propeller*

As technologically sophisticated as this folk toy seems, it was known to many so-called primitive cultures. It seems to have a nearly primordial attraction for children. This project provides a bit of a carving challenge.

(a) The propeller is shown in use.

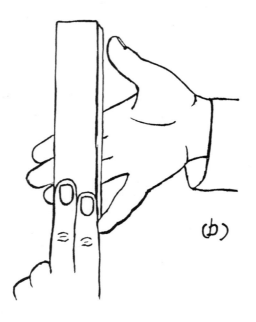

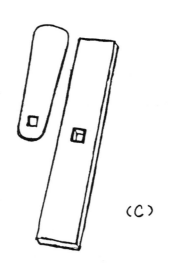

(b)

(C)

(b) Propeller dimensions:
Locate a knot-free piece of wood and relate its size to the size of the user's hand. Make the blank as long as the hand span, two fingers wide and as thick as the little finger. Small hands could find difficulty in flying a propeller that is too big.

(c) Symmetry is important:
Make a template of one blade, out of wood or cardboard. Carve a square hole precisely at the mid point of the blank. The width of the hole is about one third the width of the blank.

(d) Making the hole:
Draw guide-lines on both sides of the blank, as the hole is made most easily by working from both sides. Work the knife tip deeply in each corner across the grain only. Pry out the wood in the hole by driving the knife tip in, parallel to the grain.

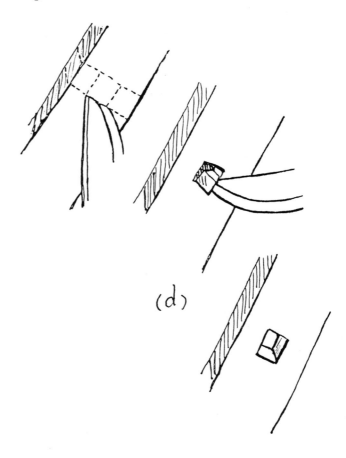

(d)

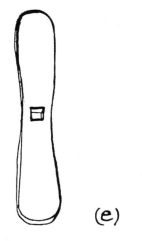

(e)

(e) The outline of the propeller is carved.

(f) **End view of the blade**:
The blades of the propeller are roughed out. If some bulk is left at the ends of the blade the added inertia will cause the propeller to spin longer.

(g) **Propeller weight**:
Except for the tips of the blades, the lighter the propeller, the higher it will fly. Contrary to popular opinion, supporting the work on the chest as shown is a safe and convenient carving stance.

(h) **Balancing**:
Press the knife blade lightly into the wood precisely at the mid-point of the propeller to mark the balance point. Keep shaving wood from the heavier blade until a balance is achieved.

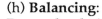

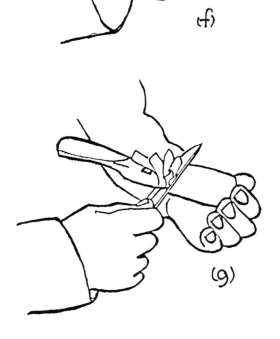

(g)

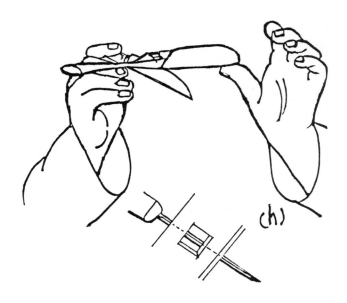

(h)

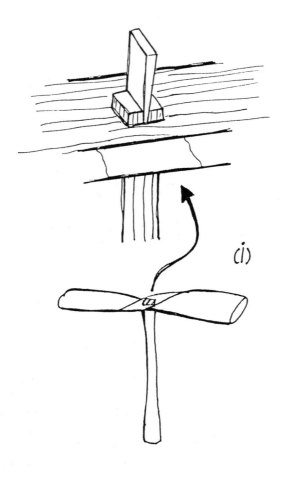

(i)

(i) **The handle**:

The handle should be about as long as the propeller. The thinner the handle the greater the spin that can be imparted to the propeller, but if the handle is too thin it may not be gripped well enough with the palms. If the handle is too light or it is crookedly put on, the propeller will wobble instead of flying. The handle is firmly attached to the blade with a wedge as shown. The wedge must part the split in the handle in line with the blade. Driving it in the other way will simply split the blade. If the wedge is too wide for the hole it could also split the blade. Trim off whatever protrudes from the hole, and the propeller is ready for use. If the propeller does not fly straight, remove a little weight from whichever blade appears to be heavier. If this begins to have the desired result, continue working on the same blade.

9 Some Spruce Root Projects

Spruce roots, as well as the roots of the other conifers, are a relatively unknown and unexploited crafting material. The roots are easiest to gather in areas of deep moss where there is no other vegetation to get in the way. The moss is pulled back to expose the roots which will be going in all directions. The roots must be followed and released carefully from the moss: pulling on a root either breaks it or those crossing over it.

The roots are stored in a plastic bag to keep them from drying out. If they dry out with the bark still on them, they will be very difficult to peel. However, unpeeled roots can be kept for a long time if immersed in water.

Roots peel most easily when the sap is rising, from mid-May to mid-July. Most often, the roots are peeled as soon as possible after they are gathered, trimmed of any rootlets and split where necessary. The roots are made up into individual coils and allowed to dry. They can be stored in the dried state for many years. When needed the roots are boiled until supple, or soaked for a day or so. This initial drying and boiling may increase the strength of the root two- or three-fold over the fresh roots. The roots neither stretch on soaking nor shrink on drying. The unique property of the root is its flexibility when supple and its inflexibility when dry.

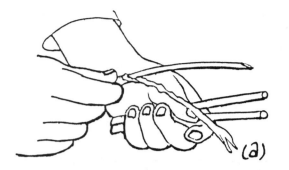

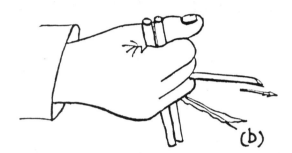

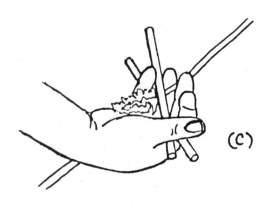

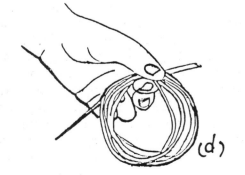

Peeling Spruce Roots:

(a) Peel a small portion of the thick end of the root with the fingers.

(b) Squeeze the root as shown between two sticks and draw the root through. Squeezing too hard may split the root.

(c) The accumulated root bark may have to be removed on occasion before peeling is continued.

(d) The ends of the root are trimmed and pointed and any rootlets cut off.

The Spruce Root Ring

The ring: The spruce root ring shown below has many applications. It can be a finger ring, a wrist bracelet, a napkin ring, a woggle, a barette, a tool handle ferrule, a knob on a basket lid or a decoration on a walking stick.

The most popular craft with young people is the ring for the finger.

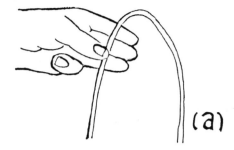

The steps in making the standard ring:

(a) Work at the middle of your root.

(b) Go around and cross.

(c) Go around again and cross as shown.

(d) Make the first tuck, on the upper part.

(e) Cross with the lower part.

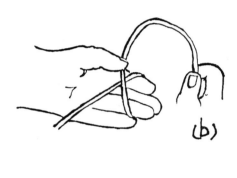

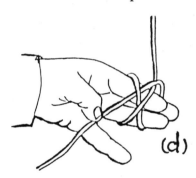

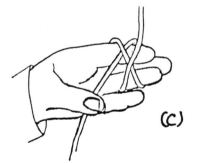

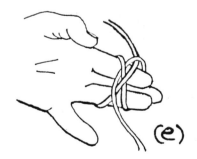

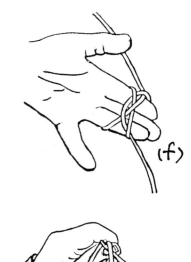

(f) Tuck on the lower part.

(g) Take the ring off the fingers and turn the far side toward you. Like a three-element braid, the part on the left passes over the part in the middle.

(h) Tuck to the left.

(i) The tuck is completed.

(j) The other end goes in beside, but in the opposite direction to, the tuck in (i) to complete the first round. If you have done everything correctly you should find that you have made a braid in a circle. If you are having any difficulty with this, practise a bit of braiding, both overhand and underhand. From one aspect the ring braids overhand and from the other aspect it braids underhand.

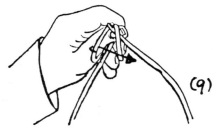

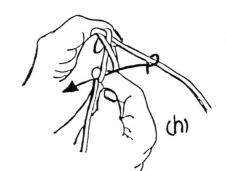

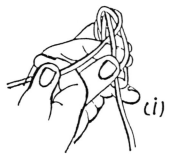

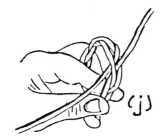

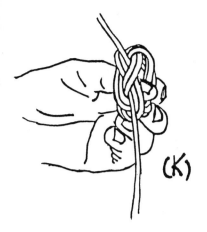

(K)

(k) Staying on one side, trace carefully with either end until the braid is doubled. The triple element ring is the most popular. It is neither too narrow nor too wide.

(l) **The spruce root coaster:**
At the single element stage at (j) flatten out the ring so that it takes the shape shown.

(m) The three-element spruce root coaster completed.

(n) **The use of the mandrel:**
A mandrel is a tapered stick on which a ring can be made to more precise size. The three element ring is started about a quarter diameter larger than the finger it is meant to fit. The mandrel is brought alongside the finger until a point is found that is a quarter diameter larger. This is the point where the ring is started. At step (g) the ring is removed from the mandrel and completed in the usual way. The finished ring is then put back on the mandrel and forced as far on to it as possible. It is pounded to flatten the braid and then pushed farther onto the mandrel. If the ring is allowed to dry on the mandrel it will be quite smooth on its inside surface.

(l)

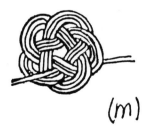

(m)

(n)

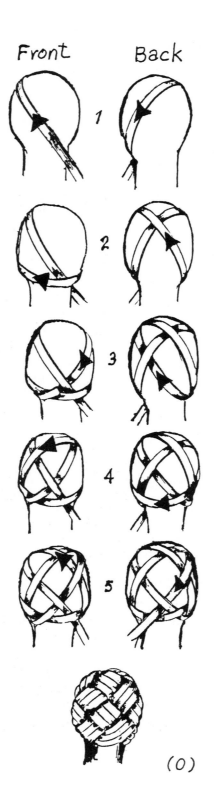

Front   Back

1

2

3

4

5

(O)

(o) **The spruce root knob knot:**
This is a decorative knot that may be used on the end of a walking stick or the butt of an awl handle. The diagrams are self explanatory.

(p) **The spruce root barette:**
This is a knot that is known as the carrick bend. It is made with supple roots and allowed to dry before use.

(p)

10 *Indian Head Carving*

A simple carving project that is very popular is the carving of a head or face. It is further simplified if the profile half-face is carved. The carving described in this chapter takes less than ten minutes to execute. With a few basic directions a fairly passable face can be carved.

(a) **The material**:
A large black poplar is shown in the photograph. Black poplar bark is an easy material to carve, but the bark on living trees is so difficult to remove that it is not worth the effort. If the tree has been dead for a few years, however, the bark may come off so easily, and in such big pieces, that the gatherer may be injured.

(b)

(c)

(b) **Preparing the bark:**
A solid piece of bark is chosen. Any loose layers are sliced away and the back of the bark is carved smooth.

(c) Determine where the top of the head and the chin are to be located.

(d) **Placing the eyebrow:** The eyebrow is approximately half way between the top of the head and the chin.

(e) **The profile:** Ignoring everything else carve the profile. The hair line is about half way between the top of the head and the eyebrow. The nose takes up half the distance between the eyebrow and the chin. The bottom lip is usually half way between the nose and the bottom of the chin.

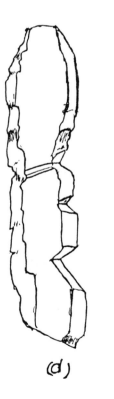

(d)

(e)

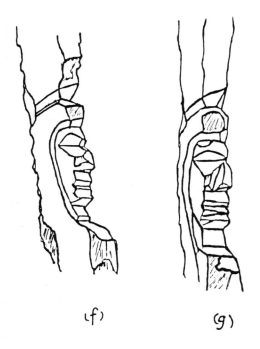

(f)   (g)

(f) **The hair line**: Delineate the hair line in such a way that the ear is hidden. Emphasize the eye socket.

(g) **Delineate the nose**: This line should run from the corner of the eye to the angle of the jaw.

(h) **The cheek bone**: The face is narrowed down from the eye socket to the jaw.

(i) The corner of the mouth is extended to the line from the corner of the eye to the angle of the jaw.

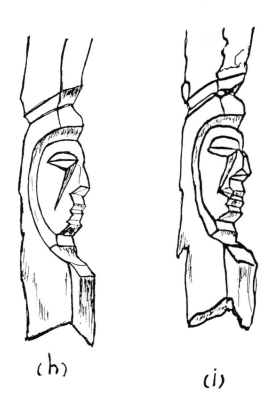

(h)   (i)

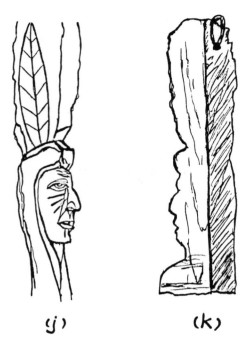

(j)

(l)

(j) The pupil of the eye is directly above the corner of the mouth. Any sharp features are rounded out, and the carving is complete.

(k) Bevel the back as shown to give the figure more of a three dimensional effect as it hangs on the wall. To make a hanger, drill a hole, insert the ends of a loop of string into the hole and drive in a peg.

(l) The top part may be cut off and a carved or real feather incorporated in to the figure.

(m) A head-dress may be made from carved or real feathers. Grouse tail feathers are very effective for this purpose.

(m)

(k)

Conclusion

A common way to enjoy the out of doors is to go for walks, to see what is happening in the local natural environment. Some of us never tire of this activity, season after season, year after year. We watch for the birds, the squirrels, the chipmunks and the insects. The flowers, shrubs and trees undergo continual changes of colour, texture and shape, providing a panacea for eye and soul. There is a certain disorder underlaid with a powerful order which provides the landscape artist with the compulsion to capture for us the scenes we do not have the opportunity to view for ourselves.

Similarly, an objective of the natural crafter may be to include some of nature's resources, so that the occasional glimpse of it will stimulate in us a basic appreciation and enjoyment. My cattail doll reminds me of the swamp that teems with life: its fertile mud; the song of the red winged blackbird; the reflection of clouds in the still water. It reminds me of the fascination that swamps had for me in my youth and the hours that I have spent in them, which account for months of my life.

A machine-made craft may be perfectly rendered. In its perfection it seems to communicate its lack of uniqueness as we are sure thousands were made exactly like it. A hand-crafted work of art, by contrast, is most highly valued for its uniqueness.

Bringing out the best qualities of natural materials is a skill that comes with practice. In the early learning stages, vary your work until you begin to acquire a form of expression which seems comfortable as well as unique to you. Try not to do the same thing twice and file away for future use the experiments which seemed particularly successful.

It is hoped that this book has introduced you to a few satisfying crafting experiences and perhaps has given you a new perspective on the natural environment. Locked up within natural materials and objects is a tremendous amount of delight for both the creators and the lovers of natural crafts. It is hoped that *Bush Arts* has been a key that fits this lock.

About the author

Mors Kochanski is author of the Canadian bestseller *Northern Bushcraft*, now expanded and in its second printing. He is former editor of *Alberta Wilderness Arts and Recreation*, and is an assistant professor in the faculty of Physical Education at the University of Alberta.

A popular speaker and instructor, Kochanski is recognized throughout western Canada for his work in the outdoor education and wilderness recreation fields. He lives in Edson, Alberta.